CW01187819

HANDBOOK FOR THE DIAMOND COUNTRY

collected shorter poems
1960-1990

HANDBOOK *for* THE DIAMOND COUNTRY
Collected Shorter Poems 1960–1990

KENNETH WHITE

MAINSTREAM PUBLISHING

The publisher acknowledges subsidy of the Scottish Arts Council in the production of this volume.

Copyright © Editions Grasset et Frasquelle, 1983
First published in France as *Terre de Diamant*
Published in Great Britain in 1990 by
MAINSTREAM PUBLISHING COMPANY (EDINBURGH) LTD
7 Albany Street
Edinburgh EH1 3UG

No part of this book may be reproduced or transmitted in any form or by any other means without the permission in writing from the publisher, except by a reviewer who wishes to quote brief passages in connection with a review written for insertion in a magazine, newspaper or broadcast.

British Library Cataloguing in Publication Data
White, Kenneth
  Handbook for the diamond country : collected shorter poems 1960-1990.
  I. Title
  821.914

  ISBN 1-85158-284-3

Typeset in 10/11 Garamond by Novatext Graphix Limited, Edinburgh
Printed in Great Britain by Martin's of Berwick, Berwick-Upon-Tweed

For the land, the light, the mind

FOREWORD

The poetry of Kenneth White

What other poet gives us this clarity, emptiness, purity of spirit, eye for the same spirit in Asia, woven with China and Tibet, a north of the soul, a pathless path? Actually it is poetry of the one world appearing and disappearing as we paddle through the sky-sea of eternity. Done with such grace and warmth, in fact. But I say too much.

Gary Snyder 4. IX. 89

TABLE OF CONTENTS

Preface.. 13

Scotland Poems

Morning walk 17
When the frost came to the brambles 18
Near Winter 19
Listening to the wind... 20
Climax... 21
Poem of the white hare 22
Winter wood... 23
On the moor in January 24
Autobiography 1.. 25
At the Great Gate 26
Chant... 27
Glasgow.. 28
Irish rain.. 29
Living in the hills 30
New moon.. 31
The western gateway 32
Report to Erigena.. 33
The territory... 34
Beinn Airidh Charr 35
Rosy quartz 36
Heron of the snows.. 37
McTaggart 38
Crab Nebula... 39
Temple near snowy mountains........................... 40
Little pelagian poem 41
Crossing Lochaber 42

For MacDiarmid	43
In the great monotony	44
Early morning light on Loch Sunart	45
Winter letter from the mountain	46
Dream ground	47
Family alchemy	48
Mountain and glacier world	49
Near point of Stoer	50
The most difficult area	51
Into the whiteness	52
Pool poem for MacCaig	53
Kenkô	54
Coastline	55
Example	56
Sun yoga	57
Road fragment	58
A short lesson in Gaelic grammar	59
Out and down	60
In a café at Largs	61
The study at Culross	62
Reading Marpa in the Blue Mountains	63
The books at Lismore	64
Letter to an old calligrapher	65
Rannoch moor	66
Obscure	67
Late December by the Sound of Jura	68
Abandoned house	69
Passing by the university in Glasgow	70
Walls	71
Strathclyde	72

Round North again 73
Late Summer journey 74
Ludaig jetty 75
Last page of a notebook 76
A high blue day on Scalpay 77

Open World Poems
Xenophanes of Kolophon..................................... 81
The wandering Jew 82
Rue d'Ecosse... 83
Drinking green tea in the rue St Antoine............ 84
My properties 85
Intellectual gathering.. 86
Gujarati 87
The absolute body... 88
Autobiography 2.. 89
Culture telegrams 90
On the plains 91
Message 92
Aurillac.. 93
Relay station 94
Fossil 95
South roads, Summer 96
Winter morning train.. 97
Café du midi 98
Nameless... 99
No four-star hôtel 100
The white mistral... 101
Salita delle Battistine 102
Found on the shores of the Black Sea 103

Europe in the Fall	104
The last days of the academy	105
Five little Greek ones	106
Patmos	107
Theory	108
A morning's work	109
Signs	110
Japanee	111
Signs and situations	112
Autumn departure	113
A fragment of yellow silk	114
A raw blue morning in Antwerp	115
Letter from Amsterdam	116
The end of philosophy	117
Trans-Europ Express	118
A little archaeology	119
Eastern waters	120
Autumn at Luk Wu temple	121
Stones of the cloudy forest	122
Rangoon rag	123
Knowledge girl	124
Earth dance	125
In the mountains of Taiwan	126
Kyoto in the fall	127
In the Straits of Tsugaru	128
North road, Japan	129
Joseph Martin's report	130
Way back	131
Passage West	132
Old man in Dogtown	133

Somewhere in New England	134
While reading Robert Frost	135
A snowy morning in Montreal	136
Tadoussac	137
Shaman talk	138
West Labrador	139
Another little shaman song	140
Ungava	141
Achawakamik	142
Autumn afternoon	143
Bum trip ?	144
South-west corner news	145
Equinox	146
Monte Perdido	147
Mountain study in Winter	148
Rock crystal	149
In a mountain hut	150
Prose for the Col de Marie-Blanque	151
The borderline	152
Saturday night whisky talk	153
Extraordinary moment	154
Big moon Autumn night	155
The Winter-Spring phase	156
The road of light	157
Wakan	158
Misty mornings in the South-west studio	159
A golden day on the Gulf	160
Inconspicuous lodgings	161
Blue thistle sermon	162
Arcachon	163
Sesshu	164

Brittany Poems
- Somewhere in Brittany 167
- Rue de Rosmadec 168
- Heard on the moor 169
- The old sea-chapel at Paimpol 170
- Portrait 171
- Place to place 172
- Brest 173
- Breton Sunday 174
- Ile de Bréhat 175
- Settling into yet another place 176
- Goaslagorn 177
- Getting things ready for the guest 178
- Good news from Russia 179
- A letter from Wisconsin 180
- On Millau Island 181
- Letter to Alaska 182
- Flotsam 183
- On the quay at Lannion 184
- Meditant 185
- At Gwenved 186

Notes 187

PREFACE

These poems were written around the world, from Scotland out.

The earliest are from *The Cold Wind of Dawn* (London, 1966) and *The Most Difficult Area* (London, 1968). Thereafter, they come from the French bilingual volume *Terre de Diamant* (Paris, 1983). And there are quite a few hitherto uncollected.

In his free meditation on a phrase from Heraclitus, Heidegger says this: "It is long, the road that is most necessary for our thought. It leads to that simplicity which is what must be thought of under the name of *logos*. There are still very few signs around to show us this road."

What I'm presenting here are maybe a few signs arising from one body-mind's attempt to follow that road.

To the poems themselves I've added notes (indicated in the text by asterisks). By no means exhaustive, they are there just to give a few discreet pointers. As well as providing information, they show the underlying philosophical-meditative line, which might not otherwise be evident. I wouldn't want it to be obvious, but one should know it's there. It's the string that keeps the necklet together.

Kenneth White
North Coast of Brittany
January 1990

"*Poiein kata physin* (to produce according to what manifests itself)"

(Heraclitus)

"If you follow this method, you will find seminal water in abundance, the fire of the mind will kindle, and the earth of thought will condense and crystallize."
(*T'ai I Chin Hua Tsung Chih*)•

SCOTLAND
POEMS

Morning walk

It was a cold slow-moving mist
clotted round the sun, clinging
to the small white sun, and the earth
was alone and lonely, and a great bird
harshly squawked from the heronry
as the boy walked under the beeches
seeing the broken pale-blue shells
and the moist piles of mouldering leaves

When the frost came to the brambles

Red they were and black
and the bitter frost
put tang into their sap

I took my breakfast of them
up on the edge of the forest
in mirkness and in mist

old man winter looked down at me
from a ragged fir tree

Near Winter

Let winter now come

ox-laden sky
cold spume of rivers
nakedness of moors
mist in the forest
let winter now come

the spoor of animals
blue in melting snow
the sun polished hard
birds and berries
bronzen shadow
water icy and thin
black crust of earth
hoar glint of stone
let winter now come

seaweed covers the moon
wind harrows the firth
the islands glint in fog
I fish in cold waters
my boat black as tar
the horned rowlocks
creak to the oar

let winter now come

Listening to the wind

1.
Autumn pools on the moors
of brown bitter water

there the cold sun reflects
and shudders when the rain

sweeps down over the hills

2.
The rotting carcass of a ram
horns creased and gnarled

the pelt bedraggled and heavy
the dip-mark blue on its side

like an October moon

3.
On the ridge among the stones
and rubble of the abandoned quarry

looking down over the sea
and the foam-curving islands

listening only to the wind

Climax

Loosen up said the sun
the entrails of the moon unfreezed
loosen up easy there
the earth began to turn and sweat
loosen up loosen up
easy boy
the birch wood gleamed in humid whiteness
her highness the Spring
broke out naked from a drift of snow

Poem of the white hare

A thought that leaped out like a hare
over the moor, from behind a great rock
oh, it was a white leaping hare, and
the heather a fine red world
for its joyance, just that day on the moor
 a grey day marching on the winds
into winter, a day for a sparkling sea
three miles away in the trough of the islands
a day high up at the end of the year
a silence to break your heart, oh
the white hare leaping, see the white hare!

Winter wood

So I have put away the books
and I watch the last apples fall
from the frosty trees

and I have seen also
acorns stretching red shoots
into the hard soil

and the white bark of the birches
was more to me than all the pages

and what I read there
bared my heart to the winter sun
and opened my brain to the wind

and suddenly
suddenly in the midst of that winter wood
I knew I had always been there

before the books
as after the books
a winter wood

and my heart bare
and my brain open to the wind

On the moor in January

Moor wind and snow
the roaring of nothingness in my ears
the bite of it on my skin
the craziness that takes hold of me
so I lurch like a madman
and laugh and cry
and lose all proportion

then the tree appears in its grotesquerie
black and twisted, solitary
and I hug it like a brother
more than a brother

rooted unrooted together

Autobiography 1

Each star
in its own sudden fire
blazes
or shoots
in a fast fine curve of light
over the breathing emptiness
and leaves me
alone by the rock
or stumbling
groping my way through the undergrowth
with only
the feeling of existence
as it trembles in an animal's belly

At the Great Gate

Now I shall take my boat again
and row out through the grey rain
to the cold salt blaze of the sun

I shall rock out there in the loneliness
the silence that is no man's business
till the winds open and let me pass

to the sudden crying of a hundred gulls

Chant

Birch rites
empty moors
raw skies
incredible snow

mussel beds
gull screams
lost islands
moonglow

wet woods
heron shells
crimson leaves
dark rain

hare pads
lightning flash
written rocks
begin again

Glasgow

1.
Betty's Bar the Ship Inn
Dick's Bar the Dublin Vaults

Saturday night, the Broomielaw
pink 'papers flutter at the corners

like exotic birds

2.
Queen's Dock on a Sunday morning
a noisy bevy of drunken gulls

the pier lined with pungent barrels
of sourmash bourbon whiskey

from Louisville, Kentucky, U.S.A.

3.
Thick fog over the docks
and as thick a silence

only one name of a ship
lit by green light

Sunrana, Kristiansand

Irish rain

Mother of mine for five days now
this heart has been smoking thick black melancholy

the rain is running down every hump
and there's not a bit of yellow sun in sight

I sit scraping away at this deal table
like an old angel trying to learn the fiddle

Living in the hills

The road I came by climbs to nine thousand feet
the river I crossed has many waterfalls
the path to the house is steep and narrow
in summer the brambles seal it off
in winter I stare out over the valley
the snow falls thickly through its darkness
I look in the fire and think it a dream
that once I lived in the streets of a city

New moon

These walls have grown sullen, and I
lodged between a dairy and an antique shop
between a station and a library, read
no future, live no present, sick
with a bellyful of memory, my skull
like an old tin can that rattles, yet

the sun will move northwards, rising
in the frozen heavens, and the day

will lengthen. New at the month's
beginning, the moon, on the fifteenth night
being close to earth and very full
will raise the tides like whales along the coast

       (Glasgow, 5th Winter)

The western gateway

The way out, hah — that blue-
black glower along the river then
the gold-amber flash then again
the blue-black glower long down the river
(old black tramp there and big
fat-bellied lazy white liner)
and fast cloud hung down low
over the greyblack waves with grist-
ling crests (oh the curving fall) above
them blackwinged sheerflighted gulls

And the hills then, red fern entang-
lements and thorn and wild rose and
holy-red holly amid the snow and
the trees stark hung with water —
walking there over blue ice paths the
streams rushing air driving sharp
and that light crazy-clear that
savage angelic and cosmo-demential light
that shows up the world in its nakedness
swift-changing darkly-bright realness

Report to Erigena*

"sunt lumina"

"Labour" suddenly seems exactly right
hard slogging, no facility
like learning the basis of a grammar
working your way into unknown logic

it's earth in labour makes for diamond

here on this nameless shore, knowing the work
who are the workers? who the travellers?
reality works — wonders? travel-travail

the old signs come out of the morning
the skull fills and empties with the tide
energy gathered, the first act

ragged coast, rugged, rough winds
the language bears us, bares us

rock province, roots — and lights

The territory

Up here in the white country

any tree for a totem
any rock for an altar

discover!

this ground is suicidal

annihilates everything
but the most essential

poet — your kingdom

Beinn Airidh Charr

There is a colder, clearer substance
on the other side of this ignorance

it is these hills, blazing
with a sanity that leaves thought behind
this light that is
the limit of austerity
and makes words blind

only in the brain, erratically
an icy ecstasy

Rosy quartz

Out of what storm of darkness
out of what hellish blaze
out of what torments and what changes

held at last in a crystal matrix
held at last in its own wild form
held in its own unbroken aura

came this incandescent stone
came this immaculate glory
came this idea of the earth

to illuminate the frozen sky

Heron of the snows

China, Xth century, when Siu Hi
painted his Heron of the Snows
on a Frost-covered Branch

the ungainly, cold-eyed bird
the mass of white plumage against
the grey sky, the uncouth claws

and Chuang-tzu asked: what
does the great bird see that can rise
so high in the wind? Is it original

matter whirling in a dust of atoms?
the air that gives life to creatures?
the unnamed force that moves the worlds?

on the riven branch, the heron
like the ghost of an answer
balances in the wind

and stares at the questioning world

McTaggart

What was he after there at Machrihanish
this man whose painting
the little critics said had no finish?

(that sense of windswept space
sea and sky in multiple movement
landscape seen as mindscape
the human figures
more and more transparent
till they disappeared)

if the question had been put to him directly
he would have made no answer
simply walked a little farther along the shore

Crab Nebula

In this lighted chaos I
live and move and have my being
in this mass of incandescence
the birthplace of a world perhaps
at least of a dancing star

in this lighted chaos I
no longer think or feel but am
involved in this swirling matter
the form I was no longer holding me
the form I will be not even imagined

Temple near snowy mountains

It must be hellish cold
the water's still moving round the rocks
but the trees are frozen stiff

white roof of the temple
there in the rough dark wood

and a little fellow with a big hat
walking head down along the shore

Fan K'wan painted it on silk
round about the millenium

*Little pelagian poem**

Jerome, to get rid of him, polemically
said he was heavy
"with Scotch porridge"

but was there ever
a brighter mind
a more diamond being

in all the murky history of knowledge?

*Crossing Lochaber**

The white hills
have perfect reflections

I came through Lochaber
in the dead of winter

to meet Matsuo Bashô
on the Isle of Dogs

For MacDiarmid*

Scotland in winter
wind whooming round the white peaks

I have been walking along the river Druie
by the golden pine and the silver birch
thinking of your poetry

now in the Lairig Ghru
at the heart of the ontological landscape
alone with the diamond body

In the great monotony

Walking in the great monotony
no music now or harmony

only the naked life-sense
and the wind of silence

eros and logos here conjoined
long dark-blue sea and quiet sand

a gull's wing makes a lonely sign
in the night of meanings: a dawn

*Early morning light on Loch Sunart**

While I write this
a grey heron
is standing motionless
in the early morning light
of Loch Sunart

At the centre
of a ring of silence
a grey heron
only the waters rippling
(language dare not be loud this morning)

For still words (long fallen silent)
listen (if you will) to these:
gheibte bradan fioruisg ann
a' direadh ris gach sruth
eoin an t' -sleibh gu lionmhor

A grey heron
watching, listening
in an early morning
glitter of waters —
maybe dreaming?

Fishing in nothingness
(that is one way of putting it)
here on Loch Sunart
bright falling of the year
quiet, so quiet

*Winter letter from the mountain**

In this world
always harder and more acrid
more and more white

you ask me for news?

the ice breaks in blue characters
who can read them?

I talk grotesquely to myself
and the silence answers

Dream ground

I came in a stranger's guise
over the white pathway, the moon
glared, cold rain
pitted the snow, the firs
on my thought's ragged edge
threw their shadows over mine

a light upshone in a window
see: a robin perched on a twig
amid humps of snow. The bolt
had the touch of a friendly hand
easy and strong, the door watched
between the stove and the elements

I have the warm cup in my hands
and the poker is tuning up the fire
and the dead man I live with
looks at me, questioning
and I search for a word of greeting
in the grammar of moon, rain, snow and fir

but there is no landscape, and no
language, only a ragged silence
so we sit there face to face
and listen to the falling rain…
blow out the lamp now, let
the stove burn deep in the darkness

uncover yourself to the bone

Family alchemy

When I think of them all:

a dancing rascal
a red-bearded fisherman
a red-flag-waver
a red-eyed scholar
a drunken motherfucker...

I take a look in the mirror
and I wonder

*Mountain and glacier world**

Arrived at this point
where the whiteness is manifest
here in the mountains
where the coldness my element
surrounds me with eternity

arrived at this point
the high crest of nothingness
where the "I" has no meaning
and the self is ecstatically
alone with its aloneness

shall I blow out my brains?

Near point of Stoer

Full moon
and a wind from the North

little sleep tonight

up at four
walking along
a silent shore

trying to translate
into a tongue that's known
a poem writ
in the language of stone

The most difficult area

To attain the most difficult area

pine branches golden grotesquely shaped
thrusting out from the parent stem

to attain the most difficult area

pebble smooth-led by the tide over gravel
now held in a seeing hand, complete

to attain the most difficult area

bird skeleton found this day on the moor
flight and flesh in the ultimate nakedness

to attain the most difficult area

Into the whiteness

Now I have burnt all my knowledge
and am learning to live with the whiteness naked

what I call art now is nothing made
but the pure pathology of my body and mind

at the heart of a terrible and joyous world

Pool poem for MacCaig

1. The classical pool

Not the golden, but the silver age
the clear, cool light of a distant sun
get that coolness on to the page
and your latin homework will be done

2. The gaelic pool

I'm a celtic text not yet gathered in
Duncan Ban knew me, and Rob Donn too
my gaelic tongue ripples round every stone
between Lochinver and Kylesku

3. The philosophical pool

Plato was naïve compared to me
that ideal system was one big bore
I'm about as deep as a pool can be
unsystematic, but ideas galore

Kenkô*

When he died, 8th April, 1350
fragments of writing were found
in the hermitage at Yoshida

a few poems pasted on the walls

Shôtetsu brought them together
under the title: *Tsurezure-gusa*
"Jottings made in idle hours"

Shinto, Tao, Buddha, K'ong
were all present in this monk's mind:
"O, characters traced by my brush
guide me at length to the pure land"

Coastline

Write poetry?

rather follow the coast
fragment after fragment

going forward

breathing

spacing it out

Example

As a thin blaze of quartz in sandstone
has behind it the whole of geology
and in its purity is beyond perfection

Sun yoga

So much has gone
now there is only the sun

the sun up there
white-golden, bare

maybe not free
but full of its own necessity

it's a world-morning
and I sit here rock-like breathing

breathing toward the sun

Road fragment

My thanks for this handful of April days
for the white wind blowing
for the dark earth and the tangled grass
and the girl beside me walking

      (Twelve Ben Country, Ireland)

A short lesson in Gaelic grammar*

The small stone is white
(*tha a' clach bheag ban*)
the white stone is small
(*tha a' clach bhan beag*)
the stone is small and white
(*tha a' clach beag, ban*)

the small stones are white
(*tha na clachan beaga ban*)
the white stones are small
(*tha na clachan bana beag*)
the stones are small and white
(*tha na clachan beag, ban*)

Out and down

Making out of town
to the end of the macadam
where old bracken spreads
darkred in the rain
and thorn grows loosely
in ragged heaps

let me lie here awhile
in the wet and the wilderness
watching
the grey cloud passing
saying a quiet hallo
to a bedraggled sparrow

*In a café at Largs**

in memoriam Pound

Blue morning
sea like glass
gulls

"came Neptunus
     his mind leaping
          like dolphins"

the little Filipino waitress
brings me another cup of coffee
with a smile on the side

"these concepts
the human mind has attained"

and the others — still
to be attained

The study at Culross

The lower room is full of objects
history's ordered bric-à-brac
in which visitors inherently bored
show intelligent interest

The upper room is still empty
there (in that small cartesian cell)
remains the merest chance
for the essential to happen

Reading Marpa in the Blue Mountains*

When the tiger year was ending
weary of the things of the world
I came to the sanctuary wilderness

the elements of wind and water seethed
the dark hills were clad in white

I don't philosophize but I keep at my task
I sleep little and meditate often

when named I am the man apart

*The books at Lismore**

Ten roaring ballads
relating to the life of Finn

fifty lochside lyrics
in very tricky measures

and a handful
of rank indecencies

Letter to an old calligrapher

A hundred days
along shore and mountain

with eye open
for heron and cormorant

now writing this
at the world's edge

in a silence become
a second nature

coming to know
in brain and in bone

the path of emptiness

Rannoch moor

Sheep trintles
a wisp of wool
buzzing fly

Obscure

Golden eagle
red deer
would be
almost too much

I'll settle for
this arctic moss
on the rock's
obscure face

*Late December by the Sound of Jura**

Red bracken on the hills
rain snow hail and rain
the deer are coming down
the lochs gripped in ice
the stars blue and bright

I have tried to write to friends
but there is no continuing
I gaze out over the Sound
and see hills gleaming in the icy sun

Abandoned house

About to draw the blinds
I see over the rooftops
and the ten thousand chimneys
with the night-fog
settling down over the city
a dark, red sun

    (Glasgow, 9th winter)

*Passing by the university in Glasgow**

"Where" cried the Ivory Gull
"where will they find it now
une forme sienne une forme maîtresse"
skimming low over Fidra in April
("maybe in the Study at Culross"
said the Long Ghost "or maybe
at St Andrews by that tower and window
or maybe on any island")

"And where are the *beaulx livres*
the *beaulx livres de haulte graisse"*
cried a fat rabelaisian Laughing Gull
dropping skite over University Avenue
("maybe in the Canongate" said the Long Ghost
"maybe in the Gorbals
maybe even, God knows, in Aberdeen
anywhere a soul has richly ripened")

"And where" cried the Rosy Gull
le cerveau ivre d'une gloire confuse
"where are the words both complex and simple
saying actual relations to the universe"
("maybe where the tree stands on the moor"
said the Long Ghost "where the rock
has its hold in the sea, anywhere
that highest intellect meets wildest nature")

"Where" cried the gulls "where"
                                      "maybe" said the ghost

Walls*

On the first wall
was a print of Hokusai

on the second
was an X-ray photo of my ribs

on the third
was a long quotation from Nietzsche

on the fourth
was nothing at all —

that's the wall I went through
before I arrived here

Strathclyde

in memoriam William White

Early morning:
a cold light
blustering over the Firth

ten tolls
on Columba's clock

"nice morning, isn't it?"

the ferry
leaving for the islands

gulls
swarming round a fishing smack
out there
in the windy whiteness

"love dwells
along the margins of the sea
and in the mind"

Round North again*

"going back home"

1.
A blue-grey stillness
where the dark waters flow —
night of the heron

2.
That branch among the fern
was a red stag
sheltering from the rain

3.
Why did he return
to that empty island?
bog-cotton in the wind

4.
Storm brewing
the world about to fall apart —
the cormorant's black cackle

5.
A grey shore
and a battered herring-box:
Scott of Stornoway

Late Summer journey

The afternoon
washed itself out with rain
and a little rainbow
appeared above Barra
almost too good to be true

two hours later
all the blues having changed into greys
South Uist was a chain of black islands
lit coldly by the moon

Ludaig jetty

The small motorboat has puttered its way
out to the fishing
the bus has passed by
to collect the children for school
the red postal van
has delivered the mail

now here at Ludaig jetty
there is only
the wind and the light
the cry of a peewit
and the lip-lip-lipping
of grey water on white sand

Last page of a notebook*

"Fuzeshin, fuzebutsu, fuzemotsu"

A bird yell
emptied my skull

ricks of hay
lined the fields

a fishing smack
lay a quiet anchor —

it was Kyle of Tongue
on a blue morning

A high blue day on Scalpay

This is the summit of contemplation, and
        no art can touch it
blue, so blue, the far-out archipelago
        and the sea shimmering, shimmering
no art can touch it, the mind can only
        try to become attuned to it
to become quiet, and space itself out, to
        become open and still, unworlded
knowing itself in the diamond country, in
        the ultimate unlettered light

OPEN WORLD
POEMS

Xenophanes of Kolophon*

Poet and philosopher.
When the Persians invaded Asia Minor
he moved to Sicily

walking around the shore of that island
he wrote:

even if you stumble
on some rocks of the truth
you'll never know it all

he spoke of sea, wind, earth
clouds and rivers
and said that god was round

*The wandering Jew**

Miniature des Heures d'Anne de Bretagne

Comes out of the white wastes
at four o'clock in the afternoon maybe
some time in the XVth century or eternity
wrapped in a dark-blue cloak of grief
a dog there scowling at his frozen heels

looking for refuge at this French house
where the servants are busy with food and firewood
(what chance has he?) his foot is on the stair

(perhaps they will not know him? have forgotten?
it is so long ago, it would be good to stay…
perhaps this house needs a secretary?) He enters —

next day along the hedges, a blizzard blowing

Rue d'Ecosse

There's nothing much in the rue d'Ecosse
that dark little cul-de-sac —
just the full moon and a stray cat

    (Hill of Sainte-Geneviève, Paris)

Drinking green tea in the rue St Antoine

Smells good and faraway present
tea from the island
of Taiwan
three in the afternoon
soft rain falling
on St Antoine —
earth oils, mountain stillness

My properties

salutations to Michaux

I'm a landowner myself after all —
I've got twelve acres of white silence
up at the back of my mind

Intellectual gathering

I've read much Hindu literature
over the past few years
close on a hundred well-studied books
but when I stood there with the girl
in the darkblue sari
and might have been expected
in that intellectual gathering
to make some appropriate conversation
all I could think of
was the darkblue sari
and her nakedness under it

Gujarati

For years a girl like you
had walked through my mind
but in the sordid precincts
of the Gorbals, Glasgow —
you carried an ancient
Gujarat with you

When you combed your hair
I saw an art come alive
when you unclothed yourself
it was stone become flesh
and when you opened your thighs
I penetrated India

The absolute body

The absolute body wakens
puts on pants and shirt

and goes out into the streets

Autobiography 2

I've been in and out of institutions
banged a few doors

in and out of lives and loves
come away with a few scars

I've gone deeper into poetry
the space where the mind clears —

now I walk in my own image
follow me who dares

Culture telegrams

1. *Yesterday*

Move over, Plato
a problematic culture
the age of anxiety

2. *Today*

Moving to and fro
a questing culture
the age of emptiness-joyance

On the plains

All around Poitiers
flat country
and the signs of a dry Summer

grass burnt yellow
sunflowers black

the lusty troubadours
have gathered in the Sympatic Bar
where all the talk
is balls and divisions

now is the time to follow
the laconic track of the crow

Message

Not far from a place called St-Quentin-les-Anges

a roadside rest-park

on the wooden table
somebody's scratched five letters

"world"

Aurillac

Big redwood in the park

sequoiadendron giganteum

and the statue of Arsène Vermenouze
"poète du félibre"

dusk now coming down

unfolding the
old blue sleeping bag

Relay station

In the Café de l'Univers
at St-Jean-du-Gard

(this is where Stevenson
said good-bye to the Cévennes)

6^{49}
September evening sun

OK
have another sip of honeyed wine
and let's move on

Fossil

In chalky stone

some day
God knows how many
million years ago

the claw of a bird
and *raindrops*

South roads, Summer

1.
Mid-afternoon
blue light flickering
on the silent crags

2.
Where did the wind go? —
dawn coming quietly
over the hills

      (Alpilles)

Winter morning train*

> *"Autonomous and emancipated, he travels hither and thither like a leaf in the wind of the Samskara"*
> (*Astâvakra gîtâ*)

Between Béziers and Narbonne
vineyards under frost
and a big red sun
running mad on the horizon

*Café du midi**

"Lo cors a fresc, sotil e gai"

Sitting here
in the shadow
with literature

I see Mireille
keen beauty
crossing the square

O night
please bring me
to her body bare

Nameless

Which one of the writers
ever
caught the sense of

difficult beauty's
little tits

see where she walks
there
clothed in the wind

over the white
sand

*No four-star hôtel**

My neighbour was Van Gogh

Sardines and rice
rice and sardines

with a red tomato

rice and sardines
sardines and rice

with a red tomato

The white mistral

> *"The Mistral is 'white' when it is not accompanied by clouds and precipitation"*
> (Book of Navigation)

Beyond the turmoil
of living, loving and dying
all at once the sky clears

a white wind blowing

*Salita delle Battistine**

A room in a poor quarter
at the top of a staircase
a hundred steps high
in a steep and narrow street

"*sono contento*", he would say

Genoa: energy and clarity
a gay hard-living people
the mountains and the sea

"There are many dawns"
he had read in the Vedas
"that have not yet shed their light"

Found on the shores of the Black Sea

Ovid talking

I remember the rain at Brindisi that November
(Virgil there twenty years before
shaking with malaria
and so sick with humanity
he'd have burnt his most ambitious book)
it whispered round the inn
where we drank the last wine
and drummed, hummed and drummed
on the roof of the cabin:
Brindisi
with its homely fishing smacks
clustered in the harbour
and the long white beaches
of the Calabrian coast ...
I at that time a broken man
taking a last whiff of Italy
(the fishy quays
the olives and the cypresses)
before moving out by the narrow channel
into a grey Adriatic
that smelt only of salt
and a wind of exile
whipping the sails —
but look out there in the waves
Proteus, the pharaoh of the seals!

Europe in the Fall

After stravaiging round the Black Sea
with a little Stambuli
I came back into Europe via Athens

rain on the olive trees
and not a living soul on the Acropolis

(where has everybody gone
where the hell have they gone —
all gone down into the plain)

I sit in an empty café
drinking Turkish coffee

looking out on the rain

The last days of the academy

By the Christian's order
the doors were closed

so they went into exile
the last seven

Damascius the Syrian
Simplicius the Cilician
Eulamius the Phrygian
Priscianus the Lydian
Hermes and Diogenes, Phoenicians
and Isidorus, who was from Gaza

they went first to Persia
then dispersed
each one, alone

walking into the emptiness

      (Athens, 6th century A.D.)

Five little Greek ones

1.
Standing at the *stasis*
waiting for the metaphor:
night ride Delfi-Athina

2.
A winter's day
on the white acropolis:
tap-tap, tap-tap-tap of the hammer

3.
All that afternoon
coming back again and again
to the thoughtful-faced Kore

4.
Under the national flag
listening (*kataresi, kataresi*)
to the pelagian wind

5.
Up on the heights —
lights coming on all along the bay:
nightfall in Thessaloniki

Patmos

Alexis signed the bull
Christopoulos the monk took it over

an island of thorn and heather
of no political interest whatsoever

books gathered there over the years
ranging from Saint John's delirium
to a life of the super-cool Buddha

Theory*

1.
The white cell almost in darkness
outside: rocks in abruption, sea-
silence wavering. It is there.

2.
Rough shape, clifted, that quartz
chaos-given, ashored, tide-washed and
in the good space gazed-at

3.
Cast — the first stone; only the
thrust and the not-silver, not-white, not-crystal
splash — no reading in the widening circles

4.
Great reason grasped, the twelve-worded orator
walks on the shingle
with quiet eyes

A morning's work

The old black man
in tattered shirt and faded blue shorts
walks up and down the beach
up and down the beach
slowly
all morning
on the lookout —
then suddenly he crouches
eyes fixed
and stalks into the sea
his net at the ready
casts it
and carefully
hauls it in:

ten silver fish
flapping in its meshes

      (near Gabès, Tunisia)

Signs

Now I've jumped off the cape
I'm lost in my own ocean

but I'm liking the swimming

for far out in the emptiness
I can see, ah, the white signs

Japanee

No longer howling city
no longer stations on the underground

the Japanee girl stands quiet there

like a blade of frosted grass
on a distant island

Signs and situations*

1.
Little Japanee apple-tree
saying quietly
no need to go to Kyoto

2.
Old Hakuin
listening to the snow
out there at Shinoda

3.
What's that? What's that?
the moon
reflected in my soup

Autumn departure

> *"Red leaves on the stream"*
> (Harumichi no Tsuraki)

Sunday morning
bright and chill
on the concourse at Orly

flight for Tokyo
via Tel Aviv
gate 50

one word to be spoken
now
for ever

if you want to know
my feelings
ask the East-flowing river

A fragment of yellow silk

Among all that display
of ancient treasure
one thing remains in my mind

a fragment of yellow silk

hardly bigger
than a breast or a hand

unearthed on the road
from Ch'ang-an to Antioch
via Samarkand

> (Exhibition, recent Chinese archaeological discoveries, Paris)

*A raw blue morning in Antwerp**

for Eloi the Slater

The rumbling of lorries
along innumerable quays

Bataviastraat, Montevideostraat

the sun's an eternally
uncut diamond

while the *Nove Anna* from Copenhagen
unloads tomato juice

Maria José counts her cash
in the Caribbean Bar

Letter from Amsterdam

It's raining
it's been eight weeks long dark raining
and I've been sitting in this empty room
listening to the rain
it's a Europe of rain
(all the bullshit of Europe
washed away in the rain)
and if I speak of Europe
it's because I'm thinking of India
looking at a photograph
cut from a newspaper
pinned to my wall :
the photo of a woman
an Indian woman
a pariah woman
her dark (very dark) face
lit by a smile
a very naked smile —
the WHITE LAUGHTER of Shiva

*The end of philosophy**

Snow drifting
across a window in Otterthal

snow
drifting
across a window
in Otterthal

        in Otterthal
     across a window
       drifting
          snow

Trans-Europ Express

1.
Watching the frost world
while my fellow travellers
talk about management

2.
Those three cities
would take a lot of telling
I laugh to myself

3.
A signal cabin flashes by
I hear my father
whistling in the silence

4.
Thinking of my old room:
the cup with the broken handle
that became a bowl

5.
Farther back still:
white sun shining
on the stones of the moor

*A little archaeology**

It was a white space on the map

Fa-hsien came by there
on his way to India
likewise Hsûan-tsang

"the sky opens, a peak reveals itself
as though risen from emptiness, a monastery appears"

came Dutreil de Rhins, came Frédéric Grenard
finding terracotta figurines, fragments of pottery
and an Indian manuscript among the oldest we possess:

a version of the *Dhammapada* written on birchbark

Eastern waters

1.
Half fish, the thread fish
alectis ciliaris
the other half sheer ecstasy

2.
What does he see
the "Japanese big eye"?
oceanic fujiyamas

        (Hong Kong Bay)

Autumn at Luk Wu temple

1.
Twelve miles along the coast
now in the evening mist
the red gates

2.
Why did Buddha come from the West?
— a bowl of noodles
and this amber-coloured tea

3.
A temple in the mountains:
the sound of sweeping
the sound of sweeping

4.
Wind in the pines
the roof-bell tolling
through the mosquito net: the moon

5.
Leaving at dawn
after rice gruel and beans
the call of a wood-pigeon

       (Lantao Island, South China Sea)

Stones of the Cloudy Forest*

In memoriam Hsiang Pi Fêng

1.
Where the path ends
the changes begin
and the rocks appear
ideas of the earth

2.
Lying in the mist
among red rocks
admiring the lessons
of wind and rain

3.
As the old man said
up in the mountains
close to the sky
every rock looks like a lotus

Rangoon rag

I have lived in the house of Rangoon Red
watching the lotus grow
let the Rangoon music run through my head
knowing all I needed to know

    (night train, Bangkok-Chieng Mai)

Knowledge girl

"Yellow body I adore"
(folksong, Laos)

Now the great space
is all around me
and you golden flower
within me

the Eastern art I made my study
is your flesh your bones
the curve of your eye
your tongue and its tones

in the presence
of your naked breasts
religion has no reality

and the smooth beauty
of your loving belly
realizes philosophy

(banks of the Mekong)

Earth dance

Red silk
red lips
red hands
red feet

red earth
red flame
red flow
red beat

red cool
red flower
red jewel
red lustre

after
take the dancer

      (A night in the hills)

In the mountains of Taiwan

Up here
there is neither East nor West
the white heron
has disappeared in the mist

Kyoto in the fall

1.
Across the wooden bridge
in the sunset —
the evening is full of echoes

2.
Night in the ancient capital —
on the grey waters of the river
a lone white heron

3.
Red lips
in a rainy street:
the face of Autumn

In the Straits of Tsugaru

Once again, outward bound

nihilistic gulls
crying in the wind

getting up into
the North-east corner of the mind

North road, Japan*

1.
That autumn morning
on the waters of the Sumida
one lone gull

2.
At Shirakawa
no poem, no song
only the rain

3.
In the mountains
on the bank of a torrent
drinking cold saké

4.
All alone
with an old crow
in unfamiliar territory

5.
Sun
shining in a waterfall
oshara shonara

6.
Green pine
growing on the heights
century after century

7.
North country:
that bear print
on the post-office wall

Joseph Martin's report

The expedition lasted
more than 6 months
we marched 125 days

the journey
was 2500 versts long
on 600 of which
we had to hack our way
with axes

we lost
all the horses
and 7 dogs
2 men died
1 went mad

the land is beautiful

      (Sikhote Alin Mts, 1884)

Way back

Rubbing noses
across the Bering straits:
America and Asia

Passage West

In search of red America
fisher of origins

"to begin to begin again"

now up in the high North-west

smoky whiteness in the air
soul of winter
breaking out into blue yelling star

the blood leaps
the hand touches roots

the centre starts from everywhere

reality's blazed

Old man in Dogtown

In memoriam Olson

"A teeny weeny one
for the road," he said
and went out again
into the grey wind

white clapboard houses
fish bones, weather vanes
salty memories
this place, another space

old man in baggy pants
bald, gasping, lumbering
still pressing forward
with an eye to the open

Somewhere in New England

East-west afternoon:
leaves of grass
reflected in my bowl of tea

While reading Robert Frost

A running shadow
brought my eye up off the page
and there outside
enveloped in the mist
I saw a hunched-up rabbit
munching sage

A snowy morning in Montreal

Some poems have no title
this title has no poem

it's all out there

Tadoussac

Off this point
you can see whales blowing

big whales from Greenland
breasting the St Lawrence

you're no longer in Canada, friend
you're up in the white wastes
of Melville's mind
there's metaphysics in the wind!

Shaman talk

I share the spirit of running water
with the hunter and the fisherman

with the hunter
I share hare, deer and duck

with the fisherman
I share seal, whale and cod

but night and the mist
blue sky, the East and the West
and the beauty of young girls
are mine alone

West Labrador

Cold sun on the taïga
at times a faint rainbow
thick moss on the forest floor
rivers, lakes, rapids

ice on the Schefferville dirt roads
thin snow on the forest ground
Indians out prowling with 30-30s
on the hunt for caribou
hare or white partridge

Another little shaman song

There's a bear's head
and a crow's wing
at my door

I walk between
blue forest and
white shore

nobody knows
what I'm doing here
what I'm looking for

Ungava

Ever listened to the wind?
ever listened to the ice?

ever listened to the wind on the ice?

that's Ungava

the name comes
from an Eskimo word: *ungawak*

"the farthest place"

Achawakamik

Up on the edge of Hudson's Bay
between the River Severn and the River Winisk
there is a place called Achawakamik

in the Cree language, that means
"a place to watch from"

they say, on the point of dying, an old man
planted his wigwam there
so that in his dying he might see
the forests and the waters
and the breath of the great spirit

if you go up there one day
try and see with his eyes

Autumn afternoon

Big silence
here on the North Coast
a few miles up
from Thunder River

I drink the last of the whisky
watching the maple leaves
burn in the frosty light

I'm saying goodbye to something
but I don't know what

      (Gulf of the St Lawrence)

Bum trip?

They said to come to Los Angeles
but I ended up in Sacramento

back to Europe in the morning!

South-west corner news

"empty activity"

Blue misty morning
sun white thistle
can't see the mountains
but there's snow on the peaks
fell last week night
will be gleaming noon

"Egyptian tanks
crossing Suez Canal
Israeli reservists
rushing to battle"

red autumn here
in south-west corner
Pyrenean silence
privileged? absolute?

drinking tea in rice-grain bowl

somewhere somebody
has to reach the cool

(Atlantic Pyrenees)

Equinox

Those tidal days

when the thunder
talks through the rain

and a lightning beauty
flashes over the brain

Monte Perdido

Walking long hours
along the dark Ordessa

"Buenas!", "Hola!"

up to the grey mass
streaked with snow
of Monte Perdido

Mountain study in Winter

"the right position"
(Pen Chi)

1.
Like the Room of Purity and Freshness
in the Tennô Palace at Kyoto

cool working here all day
with an occasional bowl of tea or soup

clean hard line of the mountains
to keep verse and thought high and in order

2.
Rustling wind among the birches
the sun making a hole in a fir

I've opened one book after another
all along this winter

now I'm just sitting in the emptiness
enjoying the sun-filled stillness

Rock crystal

There are ninety ways up the Pic d'Ossau.

"It smells of winter," he said — a shepherd with a couple of hundred sheep to look after. Asked what day it was, saying that if you stayed too long up there (he's been up three months), you begin to have "a goat's head".

In the refuge at six thousand feet, reading: some time after his death in China, Bodhidharma was seen in the Ts'ong-ling mountains, *walking back to India with one shoe in his hand ...*

Mist came down in the afternoon, just little patches at first, lit by the sun, then gradually accumulating, till it was one great silent drifting mass. As you walked, your shadow was projected on the mist, hugely, and with an aura.

Met a mineralogist who told me of a big lump of crystal he'd found embedded in the rock at an almost unreachable place. Said he'd have to break it into fragments before he could bring it down.

In a mountain hut

Suddenly the thunder
made itself heard

then in the stillness
came the far song

of one single bird

Prose for the Col de Marie-Blanque

Winter deep in the mountains. Thick falling snow. Here at the Col de Marie-Blanque, we're walking, slowly.

"No study, no book learning, you just let it filter through the mind."

There's nothing at all impressive about the Col de Marie-Blanque. Just a little mountain pass. No place for sensational exploits. Something else.

"A reality man has the diamond of knowledge."

The path moves up through the wood: pine, oak, birch. There's nothing much to be said. We don't talk. We just put one foot in front of the other, and let the snow do the work.

"Only wolves live in the dark silent wood."

We're the white wolves of those final spaces. We love this distance, this winter light. Our life is secret. It's no longer ours.

"If the great frost has never bitten the branches, how can plum blossom be fragrant?"

When they ask me what religion I belong to, I'll say: the religion of the Col de Marie-Blanque.

The borderline

It was when we topped the rise
(late April
patches of snow still lying)
we saw them:
ten ... twenty ... seventy vultures
hunched on rocks
or hopping in for another morsel of the feed
or running heavily into flight
(the feed, that was
nine sheep and a cat
scattered there
in a heap of blood and fur) —
never had I seen
so many vultures in these hills
and to complete the rareness of the sight
suddenly
out of the sun
swooped in a *mari-blanque*
circled, carefully circled again
then came in for a bite

we hunched on rocks
about fifty yards from the birds
a face-to-face
in the silence of the mountain
before moving over the frontier into Spain

Saturday night whisky talk*

"Ueno? Asakusa?"

Eight o'clock tolling
on the Bizanos church bell

I'm thinking of a haiku by Bashô

and of a lady I did know
long long ago
in Tokyo

Extraordinary moment

I have been working all morning
from midnight till eleven o'clock

now I sit drinking the wine of Maury
watching the first snow on the mountains

I can describe neither the redness of the wine
nor the whiteness of the mountains

Big moon Autumn night

Standing on the balcony
I was saying out loud
"I love you moon, I love you moon"

like some old Zen crazy coon

The Winter-Spring phase

Eight days ago
up at the Col de Marie-Blanque
it was a frozen world
with snow drifting
over arctic conifers

this morning
from this quiet room
I look at the mountain
in the warm white
misty light
of early Spring

The road of light

1.
Port of Bayonne:
a boat loading Spanish quartz
bound for Bergen

2.
Dark, dark
a sudden flash of sunlight
illuminates the yellow whin

       (a wild walk in the Basque country)

*Wakan**

"I felt something in my mind"

This is beautiful, this is beautiful
nothing is more beautiful than this

blue light breaking in the mountains
moon going down through the rain

nothing is more beautiful than this

Misty mornings in the South-west studio

1.
Cold mist
red leaves, yellow leaves
a dog barking

2.
Village of smoke
hills wrapped in mist
mountain whiteness

3.
Young mountain peak
take off that shirt of mist
so I can see your snowy nakedness

A golden day on the Gulf

Out of Socoa in a red dawn
aboard the *Apocalypse*
(used to sail from St-Jean-de-Luz)
Cpt Michel Michelena
with a crew of Basques and Portuguese

boa viagem! boa pesca!

midday saw us way out
in the Bay of Biscay
which is here the Gulf of Gascony
amid a roaring silence

ah!
the thousand daughters of the Ocean

Inconspicuous lodgings

I've emptied this room
of all but a very few images

what remains is next to nothing

the wing of a gull
a lump of cool rock
the photo of a naked girl —

within this emptiness
my being dances

Blue thistle sermon

Blue thistle on the dunes
blue burning thistle on the dunes
its roots in sand
but sturdy as hell

the sun beats
on me and the blue thistle
this long afternoon

I contemplate the blue thistle
and the blue thistle contemplates damn all

Arcachon

Lying out on the breakwater
in the warm June sun

brown water rippling

nine oyster boats
chugging by in a line

Sesshu

After years in China
emptiness achieved
he painted
with the fewest of strokes
the hardness of rocks
the twistedness of roots

BRITTANY
POEMS

Somewhere in Brittany*

An empty road

words
on a tattered poster:

Brezhoneg
Fest-Noz jusqu'à l'aube

three sparrows
in the cold raw rain

Rue de Rosmadec

White walls and gulls
extremity
impossible blackness
rapacious solitude
the narrow garden of joyance

   (Quimper, that January)

Heard on the moor

Evening twilight
on the moors of Lanvaux:
"waste land, wan land
moor always goes back to moor"

The old sea-chapel at Paimpol

Inside
religious rigmarole
but here on the grey stone wall
austere and plain
exposed to wind and sleet and rain
the ex-votos:

In memory of Silvestre Bonnard
Capt of the sloop Mathilde
lost in Iceland

To the memory of Silvestre Camus
lost in the region of the Norden Fjord
in Iceland

the eye moves on down the beach
where, on the shingle line
bulky and black
somebody's mending a boat

Portrait

Yet another of those wild ones
was Lesquin, Guillaume-Marie
born at Roscoff, year of 1803

led a seal-hunting party
to the Crozet archipelago
(a few years ago
you could still see the
piles of lichened bones)

met his death in Valparaiso
San Francisco Street
in the house of Dona Rosalia Chulena
stabbed by a man called Marin
member of the City Guard

Place to place

1.
February wood
sound of my footsteps
on the frosted leafage

      (Huelgoat)

2.
Along the ferny road
by the chapel of the Seven-Saints
under the full moon

      (Near Lannion)

Brest

1.
Brest
midnight
in the *Dead Man's Bar*

"another shot of that lousy red!"

2.
Suddenly
here I am
in the Glasgow Road

and three mad ghosts
walking by my side

Breton Sunday

Sunday morning at Plougerneau

a gull crying over the mass

"when Finn was alive, and the Fianna
sea and moor
meant more than any church"

Ile de Bréhat

It was a man from here
told Christopher

how to get to the New World

I walk among grey stones
thinking of something without a name

Settling into yet another place

1.
In the old house
the grey sparrows
talk with the brown mice

2.
Red rocks
in the morning sun
and the calls of gulls

3.
Getting on with the job
never saying a word —
the spider

4.
White beach
on a summer morning
sea surfing up through mist

5.
Blue evening light
over Lannion Bay —
I pull out the telephone plug

6.
Misty evening on the docks:
that red-bellied fish
called "the old woman"

7.
Black, white-black, black-white-red:
a quick flight of oystercatchers
over the grey sea

Goaslagorn

Little valley
full of yellow whin
for years and years
you've been a wilderness

now the committee
of "sensitive areas"
wants to make a path through you
for people to walk on
down to the sea

okay, people
there's your path
be careful with it
(no cigarette packets, no beer bottles
no radios, please)
smell the whin
listen to the wind
go down to the sea
in peace

Getting things ready for the guest

Swab the windows
(six months of bird shit
spattered mud and salty rain)
till they're clear
diamond-clear

enter now a magpie
in Chinese: "bird of joy"
chack-chack, chack-a-chack
all over the garden

put the white wine in ice

that's it
now just sit

Good news from Russia

A birdwatcher
sends me it
straight out of Siberia

a tiny wee tin thing
(seminar badge)
at the centre

two rosy gulls on the wing

A letter from Wisconsin

It comes in an almost
illegible scrawl

from N. 85th Street
Wauwatosa, Wisconsin

and I wonder
what crazy man's written it

full of American intellectualese

"the sinews of entropy
congruency to my reality"

yet it pleases me, it
pleases me well

there's a wild coolness
back of the jargon

a man's voice in Wisconsin
in the silence under Orion

On Millau Island

There he walks
old earth-man
wrapped in weather

Letter to Alaska

This is for the Arctic Loon
the Red-necked Grebe
and the Pelagic Cormorant

for the Red-legged Kittiwake
the Gray-tailed Tattler
and the Canada Goose

for the Northern Fulmar
the Great Blue Heron
and the Tundra Swan

may they escape the black flood
may they find their way into the light

Flotsam

For Matthew Graves

On a Breton shore
this autumn morning

a plank of pine

W: 22 kilos
M: 122 x 24 x 22 mm

these data are specified

beside them
half-effaced
these words:

Captain
ship
Nagasaki, Japan

On the quay at Lannion

There they were
on the quay at Lannion
mother and daughter
selling spider-crabs

big ones, real beauts
and I said
where were those fished from
our place, she said

at Paimpol
beyond the hollow rocks

Meditant

It was the cold talk of the gulls he liked
and rain whispering at the western window
long days, long nights
moving in
to what was always nameless
(though the walls were hung with maps
and below him
lay a library of science)

Outside
at the end of that dark winter
he saw blue smoke, green waters
as he'd never seen them before
they were enough
a black crow busy on a branch
made him laugh aloud
the shape of the slightest leaf
entertained his mind
his intellect
danced among satisfactory words

*At Gwenved**

1.
Summer thunder
and a white butterfly
fluttering over the maize field

2.
Early morning storm:
rain on the petunias
fine lightning in the bone

3.
Something reddening out there
very quietly reddening —
they call it Autumn

4.
An evening at Gwenved:
the red maize field
behind it, the roar of the sea

5.
On the roof now only
one lone magpie
gazing at the mist

NOTES

The diamond country

In the yoga-tantra texts (buddhist and shivaite), you meet the figure of the *vajrasattva*, the "diamond being", who has reached, if not a total clarification of himself as body-speech-mind, at least a little light. The place where Siddhartha achieved his "illumination" is called the *vajrasana* (the diamond seat), and in the *Surangama-sutra*, we read: "Wherever one arrives at illumination, that place is like a diamond." More specifically, "the diamond country" is the name of a mandala (Tucci translates: a psychocosmogram), the *vajradhatu-mandala*, inside which the adept tries to achieve enlightened consciousness. On the perimeter of this mandala, there are eight goddesses (i.e. inspirers, invitations to becoming), four of whom are abstract and four sensual. At the centre is the "queen of the diamond country" (*vajradhatu-visvari*), or the "girl of divine knowledge" (*jnanadakini*). This diamond-queen, this diamond-girl, is "the mother of all the buddhas", but in fact there is little that is maternal about her. She is a "little mother", sometimes physically presented as sixteen years old. Hence the phrase to describe the tantric yogin: "Anonymous, he wanders in the diamond country, with a sixteen-year-old girl at his side." This girl incarnates, embodies "perfect wisdom" (*prajnaparamita*), which is often compared to a diamond. In the *Shrichakrasambhavatantra*, the yogin is advised to "see in all that surrounds him the mandala of himself as *vajrasattva*". And in the *Hwa Yen Sutra* (these notions are to be found in Sino-Japanese as well as in Indo-Tibetan buddhism), we read: "Only those who have diamond minds and who have realised the non-self can know the light." Finally, let it be said that if it is good to have these notions in mind on going through the book, it would be wrong to have them *too* much in mind: the esoteric (initiatic) content should never be allowed to overshadow or overweigh the direct sensation of the poem's reality. If you stick too close to the phenomenon (the earth, or the language), you're going to be fooled, but if you stick too close to the emptiness (the abstract meaning, the diamond), you'll be suffering from religiosity sickness. If you're satisfied with "poetry", you'll never get out on the road, never understand a thing, but if you get hung up on "wisdom", it'll go dead on you.

T'ai I Chin Hua Tsung Chih

This is the famous Chinese taoist book *The Secret of the Golden Flower*, translated first into German under the title *Das Geheimnis der goldenen Blüte* (Munich,1929) by Richard Wilhelm, who left for China as a Protestant missionary but soon gave up that activity to devote himself to the study of Chinese literature. The *Secret* is a syncretic book, bearing influences from yoga, buddhism and tantrism. It may be worthwhile stressing the fact that in this method of meditation, it's the earth and the seed that are golden — the flower itself is white (which is why it is often symbolized by snow, etc.). Cf. the ten transformations of the Shakti in hindu tantrism: the tenth, *mahavidya* (great knowledge), representing the reconstitution of unity, is Kamala, the lotus-girl, and her body is golden. Cf. also the white (seminal) flower of the *bodhicitta* (enlightened mind) in buddhism. For transcription from the Chinese, I've used the Wade-Giles system adapted by Needham.

Report to Erigena

John Scot Erigena left Ireland (it's the 9th century), no doubt because of the Viking invasions. He sought refuge in France, at the court of Charles the Bald, where he studied the work of Denys the Areopagite before plunging into his own work on *The Divisions of Nature*. The authorities of the time accused him of contravening both discipline and doctrine (his was a wild, bright mind), and his philosophy was considered as belonging to the pelagian heresy. He was condemned by the Church, which has a long memory, in 1225, four centuries after his death in 877. His phrase *sunt lumina* (there are lights) refers to those "divine apparitions comprehensible to intellectual natures" that are part integral of his philosophy. I take Erigena to be a prime example of the Celtic intellectual, and look for signs of that tradition today, the tradition of the "Scotus vagans", those whom Renan (in his *Poetry of the Celtic Races*) called "teachers in grammar and literature to all the west", "studious philologists and bold philosophers". In Frederick Artz's book *The Mind of the Middle Ages*, Erigena is presented as the greatest figure of the Carolingian renaissance and one of the loneliest minds in the history of Western thought.

Little pelagian poem

The reference is to the British monk Pelagius (about 350-430 A.D.). Until maybe the time of Luther, no one created more stir in the Church of the West than Pelagius. St Augustine's doctrinal system, based on the notion of original sin, came out victor of the debates. But it was probably not for the best. And Pelagius continued to inspire an underground thought that went, say, from Erigena to André Breton's Surrealism ("Pelagius, your head erect over all those bended brows" — *Ode to Charles Fourier*). For those who're interested, Jerome's original Latin for my "heavy with Scotch porridge" was *Scottorum pultibus praegravatus*. Jerome was sent by Augustine to keep the Pelagians in order.

Crossing Lochaber

It seems hardly necessary to present the 18th century master of haiku, but I seize the opportunity to quote his warning to poets: "No matter how perfect your technique, if your feeling isn't natural, if you're cut off from reality, you'll only produce a semblance of the real thing." If I had to live with only ten books, Bashô's *Narrow Road to the Deep North* (*Oku no Hosomichi*) would be one of them.

For MacDiarmid

My preference goes to certain long poems of MacDiarmid's, such as "On a Raised Beach", "Lament for the Great Music" and "Diamond Body". MacDiarmid's vociferations (often confused) as spokesman of a Scottish Renaissance, which gave rise to a spawn of mostly very secondary poems in Lallans, have tended to draw attention away from any real study of his finer points. Let me quote here from a little known essay of his, *Aesthetics in Scotland* (originally delivered as a lecture in Glasgow in 1950, published by Mainstream, Edinburgh, 1984): "Worst of all is the continued absence of competent modern philosophising in Scotland, and above all the absence of aesthetic thought of any such value as might realign Scotland with other Western European countries and induce aesthetic developments based on Scottish roots and yet able to withstand comparison with the contemporary aesthetic thought of other countries. The omens are not auspicious. All we can hope for, it would seem, is, as in the past, an occasional voice crying in the wilderness..." Before leaving MacDiarmid, here, I'd like to quote him on another topic: the reference to far-Eastern thought, which some people may find excessive in these notes, as in the poems, preferring to relegate what I'm saying to some "sect". MacDiarmid insists, and he is not wrong in this, on the affinity between Celtic art and the East. In that same essay on aesthetics, he shows how the East, far from being an exotic or sectarian obsession, can serve as stimulation and confirmation of the deepest and most projective indigenous tendencies.

Early morning light on Loch Sunart

The Gaelic lines quoted are from a poem by Duncan ban MacIntyre (1724-1812), White Duncan of the Songs (*Donnacha Ban nan Orain*). The poem is entitled *Oran Ghlinn Urchaidh*, "Ode to Glen Orchy", and Englished, the lines say this: "Fresh water salmon was found there, heading up every stream, and moorland birds in multitudes."

Winter letter from the mountain

In his *Vajrayana* (diamond vehicle) *meditations*, C.M. Chen has this: "In the highest tantra, wherever one happens to be, that is the mandala, whatever syllables one utters, these are the mantric syllables." It's good to keep this in mind when you hear some people who are "into the East" merely mouthing exotic formulae. The thing is, to get to the top of the mountain — and keep climbing. Into clear air.

Mountain and glacier world

Maurice Blanchot talks of "that place... that farthermost region we can designate only in negative terms as a nothingness, but a nothingness which is also the veil of being." There was no real temptation of suicide here. All I wanted to do was "blow my mind", in order to get out of mental cinema into the white.

Kenkô

Urabe Kaneyoshi, who took as his monk's name Kenkô, which is the Chinese pronunciation of the two characters *kane* and *yoshi*, was born in 1283. After occupying a minor official position at the imperial court in Kyoto, where he was highly esteemed as scholar and poet, he broke with worldly affairs around the age of thirty-five and retired to the hills. He set up various hermitages, first on Mt Hiei, later at Yoshida, and finally at the Ninna-ji temple, west of Kyoto. So, there was the hermit's life, but there was also the life of the traveller (he made trips to the Kiso region, Lake Biwa, Kôbe...), and he continued his researches into Chinese and Japanese culture, notably in the library at Kanazawa. As poet, he belonged to the Mikohidari school, founded by Fujiwara Shunzei (1114-1204), and developed by his son Teika, the man who compiled the famous *Hundred Poems* anthology, familiar to every Japanese.

A short lesson in Gaelic grammar

I do not have the Gaelic, but I've done with Gaelic what I've done with several other languages: I've read everything I could find in translation, and I dip into grammars, dictionaries, and annotated original texts now and then. The idea is to awaken things latent in myself rather than actually learn the language. Maybe essential characteristics stay longer in the bones than on the tongue, maybe you can push things farther by not settling in any one tradition. To come to that white stone, in a poem of the Gaelic poet Iain Lom (17th century) a woman is compared to a white pebble. And in a Scots poem by William Soutar (early 20th century), the poet is visited at night by a woman with fresh lips and little round breasts ("I kent her by her caller lips, and her briests sae sma' and roun'"). There's a white stone also at the centre of Chinese logic: see chapter 5 of the *Kong-souen Long*. In other words, this little linguistic poem is carrying something you might call erotic logic.

In a café at Largs

Down by Largs pier, where the boats leave for Arran and the Kyles of Bute, there used to be a café with large bay windows. When I was in the area (I spent my childhood and adolescence in the nearby village of Fairlie), I liked to sit down there early in the morning when the place was practically empty.

Reading Marpa in the Blue Mountains

In 11th-century Tibet, Marpa was called the Translator (of Sanskrit texts into Tibetan). He was the master of Milarepa and, with Tilopa and Naropa, one of the principal representatives of the "white line" and the school of the Great Gesture (*mahamudra*). The Blue Mountains are, literally, the Cairngorms.

The books at Lismore

The Book of the Dean of Lismore, a manuscript put together by James and Duncan MacGregor in the early 16th century, is the oldest known collection of Scottish Gaelic poetry. I've arranged the contents a little, but the general idea is right. Finn (the White), one of the main figures in Celtic tradition, needs no introduction. Except maybe to note, with reference to the past, that he probably goes back, way beyond historic times, to an archaic deer-cult. As to the future, I have no inclination to resurrect the Fianna, or band together some modern equivalent. But I am interested in the fact that to be a Companion of Finn, you had to sever all family and clan ties, be perfectly sound in mind and body, and know by heart the twelve books of poetry. But where are today's twelve books? Hah!

Late December by the Sound of Jura

On the west coast of Scotland, you have as anarchic a cluster of islands as in Greece. The heights of Jura, called *The Paps*, shed a kind of elemental female energy in the air. If you put that energy beside the idea of "sound" (as in the Sound of Jura), you maybe have the prelude to a poetics. In a letter Victor Segalen, the Franco-Breton poet, wrote after a talk he had had on his way back from China with the Russian sinologist Alexeiev concerning the relationship between poetry and taoism, I read this, years after writing the poem: "Inspiration is a sound of the Tao, very rare, and wellnigh inaudible.... The ideal of poetry is a deep intuition that accumulates in silence and shows itself with hardly a word being pronounced." As to Alexeiev himself, here's what he says about taoist poetic intuition in his little book on Chinese literature: "A veil of snow on a little island, that is the symbol of pure inspiration. Its whiteness in the moonlight leads to a sense of integral unity." And, here, in the same area, is Jacques Maritain speaking of certain Chinese poems: "Such poems are very condensed and concentrated, expression is reduced to the essential, allusive touches take the place of any kind of rhetorical or discursive development. But however clear these poems be, however explicit and intelligible, their meaning is somehow unlimited, or, we might say: open." I'm no Thomist, but Maritain's *Creative Intuition in Art and Poetry* (1954) was my start into the field of aesthetics.

Passing by the university in Glasgow

The French quotations in this poem are, respectively, from Montaigne, Rabelais and Mallarmé, and mean "a particular form, a master form", "fine books full of marrow" and "the brain drunk with a confusion of light".

Walls

Again, with Hokusai, the master of the floating world, there's no need of presentation. But I'll take the opportunity to quote the famous passage in which he describes his life's work, since it can stand as exemplary: "At the age of six, I was seized with a strange mania to draw all kinds of things. At fifty, I had produced a great number of works of various kinds, but none completely satisfied me. The real work began for me when I was seventy. Now, at the age of seventy-five, I'm beginning to get a real feeling for nature. At eighty I hope to have attained a certain power of intuition, and that it will develop till I'm ninety, so that at a hundred years of age I may possibly be able to say that my intuition was that of an authentic artist. And, if I was ever lucky enough to live to a hundred-and-ten, I think a deep and living understanding of nature would radiate from every line I drew. I invite all those who'll live as long as me to see if I keep my word. Written at the age of seventy-five by me, once named Hokusai, the old man crazy with painting." The name Hokusai, by the way, means "northern study". There are quite a few northern studies in this book.

Round North again

In Ch'an Buddhism, the phrase "going back home" means the dissolution of the personal ego, the experience of emptiness, the discovery of one's "original face".

Last page of a notebook

The Japanese words, whose source is the text known as *The Gateless Gate*, are a definition of absolute reality: "Neither mind, neither Buddha, nor a thing." Kyle of Tongue is a stretch of water in the far north of Scotland.

Xenophanes of Kolophon

Hardly anything is known about this pre-Socratic Greek philosopher, a contemporary of Pythagoras. All we have of his thinking and writing are fragments, but it's enough to know that he had a sharp mind, as well as a sense of humour. He spent a lot of his time on the road: "Sixty-seven years have seen my unquiet thought wandering over the land of Hellas."

The wandering Jew

Among the numerous mediaeval "books of hours", that tell the course of the year, one of the most beautiful is that of Anne de Bretagne, which dates from the 15th century. I like the lines and the colours and the atmosphere of the seasonal miniatures, less fantastic than Bosch, less boisterous than Breugel, but every bit as imaginative and vigorous. There was a clarity and an edge in those "dark ages", and the beginnings of "landscape-mindscape".

Winter morning train

What distinguishes the *Astâvakra gîtâ* from the better known *Bhagavad gîtâ* is that it shows no interest whatever in the idea of a personal God. It also livens up upanishadic vocabulary by the invention of new terms.

Café du midi

The epigraph of this poem ("Her body is fresh, subtle and delightful") is from the Provençal of Bernard de Ventadour.

No four-star hôtel

I wouldn't want to turn this poem into a heavy symbolical text (though rice, sardines and a tomato *could* signify, earth, sea and the sun ...). But that red tomato reminds me of a phrase of Walt Whitman's. He said once that with a tomato in his hands he'd walk through the world and confound all the philosophers. Maybe that's what Husserl did with his phenomenology. Walt himself was on the right road (the good red road ...), but he tended to talk too much. In Haiku country, he would have founded the Red Tomato School, and done more walking than talking.

Salita delle Battistine

The occupant of this modest but very high room is, of course, Friedrich Nietzsche.

Theory

The word "theory" in this poem may seem totally out of place. A hard-minded epistemologist will say (1) that a theory is based on observation and experience, (2) that it can be refuted or verified, (3) that its function is to render coherent and conceptualize data hitherto isolated and unexplained. Little of that in this poem. But theories, like methodologies, can be a block on thought, especially when only a certain *type* of theory, a certain *type* of methodology is entertained. Maybe this poem goes back to a more primordial sense of theory, the one still present in Aristotle when he says that life spent in theory is a kind of divine life, ontologically extraordinary.

Signs and situations

Hakuin was a Zen master, one of the best. He was ten years old at the death of Bashô in 1695, and he died at the age of eighty-four. "A wild tiger will never touch rotten meat," he said. It was because there was too much cultural rotten meat around that I went out, with Hakuin in my hand, into the cold. Hakuin is author of *A quiet Night talk on a Boat* (*Yasenkanwa*), and *The Teakettle* (*Orate Gama*). He was against "sitting meditation" (*zazen*), and went in rather for what I'd call walking meditation. Painter, calligrapher and poet, he knew what he called "the ecstasy of expression". When his time had come, he lay down quietly to die. But, at the very last moment, he let out a shout. He knew what he was doing.

A raw blue morning in Antwerp

Eloi Pruystinck, a slater to his trade, founded, at the beginning of the 16th century, in Antwerp, the group known as the Loïsts. This group continued the tradition of the *Homines intelligentiae* and the *Brothers of the Free Mind* which had started up three centuries before. Anarchists, erotic mystics, libertine intellectuals, they were looked at sideways by the Papists, and condemned by the protestant Reformers. They were really elsewhere, on other ground.

After the visit that Eloi paid him in 1525, Luther wrote a letter to the "Christians of Antwerp", telling them to have nothing to do with this *rumpelgeist*. Calvin for his part, in 1545, put out a pamphlet *Contre la secte phantastique et furieuse des libertins qui se nomment spirituels*. The Catholic mystic Suso (14th century) had a dream in which he met up with a libertine intellectual and put a few questions to him: "Where do you come from? Nowhere. What is your name? I am called nameless Nature. Where does your vision of things lead? Total freedom." It's the old forces rising up against dogma, cult and structure. To be compared with taoist and tantric groups in the East.

The end of philosophy

It was in Otterthal, it will be remembered, that Wittgenstein, during a break with philosophy (at least written, public philosophy), taught school.

A little archaeology

Fa-hsien and Hsûan-tsang were Chinese buddhists (7th century) who left for India via the Gobi desert in search of manuscripts. The best book on the cultural context and the travels themselves is probably René Grousset's *Sur les traces du Bouddha*. In it, he says of Hsûan-tsang (or Hiuan-tsang, depending on the transcriptions): "In Hiuan-tsang there is not the slightest trace of exclusivism. And therein lies his strength. Many a monk was limited to the teachings of his sect, but not so Hiuan-tsang. His familiarity with the most widely differing schools made him unbeatable in argument. In the course of his metaphysical debates with the learned doctors of central Asia and India, he was always able to outdo them thanks to the weight of his erudition and the vivacity of his quotations." Dutreil de Rhins and Frédéric Grenard were among the 19th- and early 20th-century archaeologists who explored the sites in the Tarim Valley where so many ways of life and thought came together. As to the *Dhammapada* (the "right path" in Pâli), it is an early Buddhist collection of 426 stanzas, famous both for its teaching and its literary value. That the text should have been written on birch bark may simply be due to the fact that birch was handy on the slopes of the Himalaya. But it may also be noted that in Indo-European languages, the words for "tree" have a common root, and the original tree seems to have been a birch. The birch is to northern Eurasia what the bamboo is to cultures further south.

Stones of the Cloudy Forest

Hsiang Pi Fêng had always wanted to go to the Yellow Mountain, but it was only late on in life he could fulfil his desire, after spending long years "plowing with his tongue and eating rice-gruel", that is, earning his living by teaching. He was so delighted with his experience of the mountain that he felt he had to mark the event. So he began to go through all the books he could get his hands on, looking for poems or even just simple phrases concerning Yellow Mountain. Out of these poems and phrases he made an anthology. Such a "tongue-plowman", lover of books and mountains, deserved at least a mention in this book.

North road, Japan

The words *"oshara shonara"* are from a country Nô play danced in the Yamagata, North-west Japan. Like other words in such contexts, they mean nothing (they are probably, in origin, deformed Sanskrit), but they have an *aura*. In the economy of this poem, the words represent the language of something outside my habitual consciousness, and convey, to my ear, an impression of freshness and light, also, more abstractly, primalness, firstness (all those "a"s).

Saturday night whisky talk

"Ueno? Asakusa?" This is the last part of a haiku by Bashô. He's in his hut on the east bank of the Sumida River and, hearing bells ringing, wonders if they are those of Ueno or of Asakusa, two other quarters of Tokyo.

Wakan

Among the Indians of North America, *wakan* signifies "sacred". But it's not absolutely forbidden to read also into the title of this poem the word "waken".

Sesshu

The Japanese painter Sesshu (1420-1506) did in painting what Bashô did in writing. As Su Tung-p'o said: "Poetry and painting aim at the same thing: an unmixed freshness and an effortless skill."

Somewhere in Brittany

The words on the poster are a mixture of Breton and French. *Brezhoneg* is Breton for the Breton language. A *fest-noz* is, literally, a "night festival", and this one promised to last "right till dawn" (*jusqu'à l'aube*).

At Gwenved

This notion is at the core of Celtic culture. Literally: "the white country". *Gwenved* in Brythonic (Welsh, Breton), *finn mag* in Goedelic (Scots and Irish gaelic). Used in Christian times as a translation for "paradise". But it is very much of this earth. I see it as a place of light and delight, the light, of course, not excluding darkness, the delight, not ignorant of fracture patterns.